PSYCHIATRIC
Phenomenology From First Principles for Medical Students, Psychiatric Residents, and Practitioners

DANIEL CHINEDU OKORO, MD

Psychiatric Phenomenology From First Principles for
Medical Students, Psychiatric Residents, and Practitioners
Copyright © 2022 by Daniel Chinedu Okoro, MD

All rights reserved. No part of this publication may be
reproduced, distributed, or transmitted in any form or by
any means, including photocopying, recording, or other
electronic or mechanical methods, without the prior
written permission of the author, except in the case of
brief quotations embodied in critical reviews and certain
other non-commercial uses permitted by copyright law.

Tellwell Talent
www.tellwell.ca

ISBN
978-0-2288-6972-6 (Hardcover)
978-0-2288-6971-9 (Paperback)
978-0-2288-6973-3 (eBook)

TABLE OF CONTENTS

What This Book Is Not v
Definition vii

Disorders of Movement and Behaviour 1
Disorders of Speech 6
Thought and Beliefs 11
Disorders of Perception 18
Disorders of Affect and Mood 26
Disorders of Consciousness 34
Phobias and Anxieties 38
Depersonalisation and Derealisation 41
Intelligence 43
Disorders of the Self 46
Disorders of Memory 49

Bibliography 53
About the Author 55

WHAT THIS BOOK IS NOT

This book is not a work of genius.

This book is not a comprehensive immersion into the complex world of psychodynamic and psychoanalytic phenomenology.

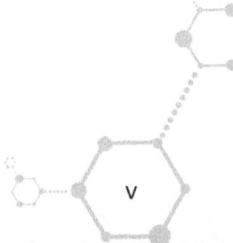

DEFINITION

What is psychiatric phenomenology?

It is just how one explains away what is happening to oneself emotionally in addition to how others describe one's behaviour and actions. Psychiatric phenomenology is also called descriptive psychopathology.

DISORDERS OF MOVEMENT AND BEHAVIOUR

AGITATION OCCURS IN THE FOLLOWING CONDITIONS:

Severe mood disturbance with or without psychotic symptoms

Schizophrenia

Major psychiatric conditions due to general medical conditions

Severe anxiety disturbance

Personality disorder

Hyperthyroidism

Hypoparathyroidism

STUPOR IS MADE UP OF:

Akinesis (lack of movement)

Muteness (lack of speech)

Stupor occurs in organic psycho-syndromes, mania, and schizophrenia.

MOVEMENT DISORDERS OCCURRING IN SCHIZOPHRENIA INCLUDE:

Catatonia – lack of movement with body held in an unusual posture

Waxy flexibility – initial resistance to being moved slowly gives way, so that the patient can be positioned in another posture where they remain, just like working on a warm candlestick

Psychological pillow – observed when patient is seen lying on their back but elevating the head as if there is a pillow under the head when there is none

Stereotypy – a pattern of non-goal-directed movement that is repetitive and follows the same format; the patient can be distracted from this movement

Mannerisms – goal directed, ritualistic, but peculiar ways of moving or behaving that need not be repetitive or follow the same pattern

Grimacing – the face is held in a distorted fashion, with twisting of the mouth

Snout spasms – the nose and lips are held in a spastic fashion as if mimicking the snout of an animal

Parkinsonian syndrome movement – includes slowness of movement, tremulous movement, muscle rigidity, posture and gait problems, loss of ability to blink or smile

OTHER MOVEMENT DISORDERS IN SCHIZOPHRENIA INCLUDE:

Negativism – moves in the opposite direction that the patient is instructed to move, or lack of enthusiasm to move, or moving at variance to intended instruction

Automatic obedience – obeys movement request automatically irrespective of consequence

Ambitendency – moves or acts in the opposite direction of the examiner

Obstruction – moves to block the intended motion of examiner

Mitgehen – slight finger pressure on the patient elicits exaggerated movement in any direction despite the patient being told not to move

Echopraxia – involuntarily repeats the movement or behaviour of the examiner

Advertence – the patient, being mindful of examiner's intended direction of motion, tends to move in that direction

Opposition – resists the desire or instruction to move

PARKINSONISM INCLUDES:

Slowing of emotional and voluntary movements

Muscular rigidity

Akinesis

Tremor

Disorders of gait, speech, and posture

TYPES OF DYSTONIA:

Acute dystonia

Oculogyric spasm

Vocal dystonia

Segmental dystonia

Drug-related dystonia

Psychogenic dystonia

TICS ARE:

Rapid movements

Repetitive

Co-ordinated

Stereotyped

Able to be mimicked

Usually reproduced faithfully by the sufferer

SOME DISTURBANCES OF BEHAVIOUR THAT MAY OCCUR IN SCHIZOPHRENIA:

Movement disorders

Hoarding

Water intoxication

Mannerisms

Gross neglect, otherwise known as Diogenes syndrome

Flagrant stealing

Unprovoked aggression and nastiness

Childishness or grotesque behaviour

Self-immolation (setting self on fire) and suicide

DISORDERS OF SPEECH

DISORDERS OF SPEECH MAY INCLUDE THE FOLLOWING:

Flight of ideas: Speech changes from subject to subject with retention of connection between the speeches. Occurs in mania.

Thought blocking: Patient will suddenly say that their mind has gone blank and they cannot complete the sentence at hand. May occur in schizophrenia.

Overinclusive thinking: There is loss of conceptual boundaries, as in schizophrenia.

Pressure of speech: There is an increase in rate of speech production, as in mania.

Circumstantiality: Speech is burdened with unnecessary information; the person making the speech may be said to be beating about the bush. May occur in obsessive-compulsive disorder.

Echolalia: The patient repeats the speech of the interviewer verbatim.

Verbal perseveration: This may include palilalia, where the patient repeats the last word, or logoclonia, where the last syllable is repeated.

Clang association: Speech connections are based on their sound. Punning and rhyming are examples.

Loosening of association: An example of this is knight's move thinking, where there is no connection between ideas. This may occur in schizophrenia. Derailment and tangential thinking are examples.

Neologisms: This means new word formation or idiosyncratic use of a word. This occurs in schizophrenia.

Mutism: A total loss of speech in full consciousness, as may occur in catatonia.

One may consider disorders of the form of speech as disorders of speech, but this is discussed under disorders of thought and beliefs.

SPEECH BECOMES UNINTELLIGIBLE WHEN THE FOLLOWING ARE PRESENT:

Dysphasia: The loss of ability to produce speech and understand spoken language.

Paragrammatism: Speech is full of grammatically incorrect sentences, as occurs in fluent aphasia/receptive aphasia.

Neologism: New word formation.

Use of stock words and phrases: The patient has poverty of words to use in speech; for example, where the patient is supposed to use Coca-Cola, Sprite, Fanta, or ginger ale in speech, they will use a stock phrase like "sweetened liquids".

Use of private language: For example, the patient may use cryptolalia when spoken and cryptographia when written. Private language in schizophrenia known as "schizophrenese" cannot be understood by others except the patient.

THE FOLLOWING ARE FORMS OF MOTOR APHASIA:

Pure word-dumbness

Pure agraphia

Alexia with agraphia

Isolated speech area defect

Mutism

SCHIZOPHRENIC LANGUAGE DISORDERS INCLUDES:

Akataphasia: Use of inappropriate or grammatically incorrect words

Loosening of associations

Regression: Loss of quality and quantity of previously acquired speech

Asyndesis: Comprising derailment, loosening of association, knight's move thinking, entgleisen, giving rise to nonsensical speech

Concrete thinking: Literal thinking, based on the "here and now" interpretation of information

Defect of deductive reasoning

Neologisms and blocking

SCHNEIDERIAN SCHIZOPHRENIC SPEECH DISORDERS INCLUDE:

Derailment

Substitution

Omission

Fusion

Drivelling

IN SCHIZOPHRENIC LANGUAGE:

There is intrusion of dominant meaning of word when the situation demands the use of a less common meaning (unintentional puns).

Neologisms are used to fill semantic gaps.

Clang associations occur with the initial syllable of a previous word (in mania and poetry, terminal clanging occurs).

Punning, clanging and ideational similarity can be provoked by a word in a clause.

Disturbances of words and their meaning are more common than disturbances of grammar and syntax.

More syntactic errors occur in schizophrenia than mania.

ACCORDING TO THE BEHAVIOURAL CONCEPT OF LANGUAGE:

Language is a learned behaviour.

Schizophrenics will give more unusual answers to stimulus words than controls.

Schizophrenics will respond to a word's dominant meaning regardless of context.

WITH REGARDS TO SPEECH:

Predictability is the ability to predict accurately the missing words in a cloze test.

Schizophrenics are unpredictable in the cloze test.

Type-token ratio is lower in schizophrenics since more token words are used.

PSYCHOGENIC SPEECH ABNORMALITIES IN SCHIZOPHRENIA INCLUDE:

Flight of ideas

Pressure of talk

Hysterical mutism

Approximate answers

Paraphasia

Pseudologia fantastica

Eccentric and pedantic use of words

THOUGHT AND BELIEFS

OBSESSIONS:

Obsessions are recurrent, intrusive, persistent thoughts, urges, or images that are unwanted and cause marked anxiety and distress. The patient believes these thoughts, images or impulses are theirs and not alien. Because they are distressing, they are therefore ego dystonic. A patient with obsessional imagery and thoughts of throwing down their baby from the 10th floor window of their apartment is so heavily distressed by this thought that they are very unlikely to harm their baby. They will stay away from the window and actively seek help for their anxiety. However, a mother who believes the baby is a reincarnation of the devil and hears a voice telling her to throw down the baby is likely to obey the voice and harm the baby, and hence, in delusions, the feelings are ego syntonic.

Obsessional themes include contamination, doubt, safety, symmetry, religion, illness, sex, violence, and so on.

Ritualistic behaviours called compulsions accompany the obsessions in an attempt to neutralise the obsessional anxiety.

FORMAL THOUGHT DISORDER IS ABNORMALITY IN THE MECHANISM OF THINKING. IT INCLUDES:

Acceleration of thinking

Retardation of thinking

Circumstantial thinking

Thought blocking

EXAMPLES OF FORMAL THOUGHT DISORDER:

Crowding of thought

Perseveration

Concrete thinking

Fusion

Derailment

TYPES OF THINKING:

Fantasy or dereistic or autistic thinking

Imaginative thinking

Rational or conceptual thinking

FANTASY THINKING OCCURS:

In daydreams

As a way of life

In shy, reserved people

In schizophrenics

THE FOLLOWING REVEAL FANTASY THINKING:

Pathological lying

Hysterical conversion and dissociation

Delusion-like ideas

Slips of tongue

Forgetting an emotionally laden word during a speech

THE PSYCHOLOGICAL THEORIES OF SCHIZOPHRENIC THINKING INCLUDE:

Asyndesis manifesting as overinclusive thinking

Broadening of category boundaries

Kelly's personal construct theory using the repertory grid, which suggests that schizophrenics have a personal way of interpreting and predicting events going on around them.

Kelly, G. (1955). *The psychology of personal constructs* (Vols 1–2). New York: WW Norton.

THE THREE COMPONENTS OF A DELUSION, ACCORDING TO JASPERS, ARE:

Belief held with unusual conviction

Belief not amenable to logic

Belief is absurd and erroneous to other people

Jaspers, K. (1959). General Psychopathology (transl. Hoenig J and Hamilton MW, 1963). Manchester University Press.

THE PROPERTIES OF A DELUSION ARE:

Falsity

Unshakeability

Out of keeping with the cultural background

Held with extraordinary conviction and subjective certainty

Like a true belief to the patient

EXAMPLES OF FALSE BELIEFS:

Primary delusion

Secondary delusion

Overvalued ideas

Sensitive ideas of reference

THERE ARE FOUR TYPES OF PRIMARY DELUSIONS:

Delusional perception (there is a normal perception that the patient gives a delusional false interpretation to)

Delusional intuition

Delusional atmosphere (mood)

Delusional memory

PRIMARY DELUSION:

Is an autochthonous delusion arising de nuevo, out of the blue

Is un-understandable

Occurs in the absence of any other psychopathology

According to Cutting, occurs in schizophrenia and not in any other condition

Cutting, J. (1985) The Psychology of Schizophrenia. Edinburgh: Churchill Livingstone.

EXAMPLES OF DELUSIONS ARE:

Delusion of persecution

Delusion of jealousy

Delusion of love

Delusion of misidentification

Delusion of grandiosity

Religious delusion

Delusion of guilt

Delusion of nihilism (in an extreme form known as Cotard's syndrome, the patient believes they are dead, nonexistent, and rotting)

Delusion of hypochondriasis

Delusion of infestation (Ekbom's syndrome)

Delusion of control

Communicated delusion (folie à deux)

PROPERTIES OF AN OVERVALUED IDEA:

Acceptable, understandable

Pursued beyond bounds of reason

Neither delusional nor obsessional

It is not senseless to the patient

It has the quality of a passionate political or religious conviction

The patient may invariably act on the idea

EXAMPLES OF OVERVALUED IDEAS:

Litigious type of paranoid states

Morbid jealousy

Hypochondriasis

Dysmorphophobia

Parasitophobia

Anorexia nervosa

FIRST RANK SYMPTOMS:

There are eleven first rank symptoms. They are not diagnostic of schizophrenia or any other condition. They can occur in any other condition apart from schizophrenia.

Their presence is strongly suggestive of schizophrenia. They are made of three hallucinations, three thought phenomena and four passivity or made experiences and delusional perception.

Voices running a commentary on patient's actions in the third person (e.g., "He has just left", "He has put down his plate")

Voices discussing or arguing among themselves about the patient

Thought echo, whereby patient hears his thought spoken out aloud

Thought insertion

Thought withdrawal

Thought broadcast

Made actions

Made feelings

Made impulses

Somatic passivity: Sensations are imposed on the body by an external force

Delusional perception

DISORDERS OF PERCEPTION

THERE ARE TWO TYPES OF ABNORMAL PERCEPTION:

Sensory distortion

False perceptions, which include illusions, hallucinations and pseudohallucinations

SENSORY DISTORTION MANIFESTS AS:

Changes in intensity and quality of perception or the spatial form of the perception

Changes in the feelings associated with perception

Splitting of perception

ILLUSIONS:

Are transformations of perceptions

Types are completion, affect and pareidolic

Fantasy (imagery) plays a role in formation of illusions

Paying attention to a completion illusion makes it disappear

Completion illusion demonstrates the principle of gestalt psychology

PAREIDOLIC ILLUSIONS:

Could occur in normal people

Images are seen from shapes

Are not banished by attention (vs completion illusion)

Paying attention to the illusion increases its intensity

Are more common in children

SLADE'S THREE CRITERIA FOR HALLUCINATIONS:

It is a percept-like experience in the absence of an external stimulus

It has the full force and impact of a real perception

It is unwilled, it occurs spontaneously, and it cannot be readily controlled by the patient.

Slade, P. D., & Bentall R. P. (1988.) *Sensory deception: a scientific analysis of hallucinations*. London: John Hopkins University Press.

REGARDING AUDITORY HALLUCINATIONS:

Elementary (unstructured) sounds that occur in organic states are unpleasant and frightening

Phonemes (voices) occur in schizophrenia, chronic alcoholic hallucinations, and affective psychosis

In schizophrenia, thought echo, commentary voices, or voices discussing with each other may occur

May be abolished by wearing ear plugs

Paying attention to distracting noise diminishes auditory hallucinations

STRATEGIES THAT HELP WITH COPING WITH AUDITORY HALLUCINATIONS ARE:

Change of posture of spatial position

Relaxation and physical exercises

Control of attention, active suppression of hallucination, and cognitive reappraisal

REGARDING VISUAL HALLUCINATIONS:

Occur in organic states, including occipital, temporal, and parietal lobe tumours

May occur with dyslexia

May occur with cortical blindness

OTHER CONDITIONS GIVING RISE TO VISUAL HALLUCINATIONS ARE:

Post-concussion states

Epileptic twilight states

Metabolic disturbances

Alzheimer's disease

Huntington's chorea

Multi-infarct dementia

Recreational drug use

VISUAL HALLUCINATIONS:

Are uncommon in schizophrenia

Do not occur in uncomplicated mood disorders

In schizophrenia, auditory hallucinations may be commonly associated with visual pseudohallucinations

Are vivid and elaborate in oneiroid states where there is coexistent alteration of consciousness

CHARLES BONNET SYNDROME:

Phantom visual images occur

Visual hallucinations are complex

There is absence of psychopathology

There is no disturbance of consciousness

Occurs at any age

More common in the elderly

Associated with central or peripheral reduction of vision

Could last from days to years

The images could be static, moving, or animated

IN AUTOSCOPIC HALLUCINATIONS:

Patient sees an image of themselves in external space

More common in males

Neurological and psychiatric disorders occur in 60% of patients

Epilepsy occurs in 33% of patients

Most common psychiatric diagnosis in people showing autoscopy is depression

Episodes of autoscopy last less than 30 minutes

Fear and anxiety are provoked

HALLUCINATIONS OF BODILY SENSATIONS:

May be superficial, kinaesthetic, or visceral

Superficial hallucinations include thermic, haptic, and gyric hallucinations

Are common in schizophrenia where they are elaborated as delusions of control

REGARDING OLFACTORY AND GUSTATORY HALLUCINATIONS:

Frequently occur together

Associated with powerful emotions

Occur in schizophrenia, epilepsy, and organic states

Temporal lobe epilepsy is associated with hallucinations in all sensory modalities

PSEUDOHALLUCINATIONS:

Are figurative

Are not concretely real

Are experienced in inner subjective space

May have definite outline and vivid detail

Cannot be deliberately evoked

Are experienced as an "as if" experience

PSEUDOHALLUCINATIONS OCCUR:

In normal people

In bereavement as a hallucination of widowhood/widowerhood, which can be reassuring and helpful

EXTRACAMPINE HALLUCINATIONS OCCUR:

Outside the limits of sensory field

In schizophrenia

In epilepsy

In organic states

In normal people as hypnagogic (when going to bed) or hypnopompic (when rising from sleep) hallucinations

HYPNAGOGIC (WHEN GOING TO BED) AND HYPNOPOMPIC HALLUCINATIONS (WHEN RISING FROM SLEEP):

Occur in normal people

Occur in narcolepsy

Occur in sleep paralysis

Occur in toxic states

Occur in phobia

Are of sudden onset

May be visual, auditory, or tactile

FUNCTIONAL HALLUCINATION:

A real external stimulus is needed for the functional hallucination to occur

Both the stimulus and the hallucination are in the same modality (e.g., a sound like running water will prompt the auditory hallucination)

Above occur simultaneously

REFLEX HALLUCINATION:

Is a hallucinatory form of synaesthesia

A stimulus occurs in one modality

In response, a hallucination occurs in another modality

An example: A patient hears a certain word in a normal conversation but feels pain as a result

DISORDERS OF AFFECT AND MOOD

JASPERS CATEGORISED EMOTIONS ACCORDING TO:

Object of emotion

Source of emotion

Biological purpose

Duration and intensity

Emotion and sensation

Jaspers, K. (1963). *General Psychopathology*, 7th edition (J. Hoenig and M. W. Hamilton, Trans.). Manchester: Manchester University Press. (Original work published 1959)

THE PATHOLOGICAL CHANGES IN MOOD ARE:

Loss of feeling of capacity

Increased feeling of capacity

Absence, blunting, and flattening of feeling

Anhedonia

Feeling of impending disaster

Ecstasy

Investing of idiosyncratic affect on any object of perception

Change of affect towards people

Ambivalent affect

Free-floating emotion

Hypochondriasis

ALEXITHYMIA:

Difficulty in verbalising affect

Difficulty in elaborating fantasy

Reduction in symbolic thinking

Literal thinking

Stiff robot-like existence

Cannot empathise

ALEXITHYMIA CAN BE FOUND IN THE FOLLOWING CONDITIONS:

Psychosomatic disorders

Somatoform disorders

Psychogenic pain disorders

Substance-use disorders

Post-traumatic stress disorder

Masked depression

Neurosis

Sexual perversion

IN MAJOR DEPRESSIVE DISORDER:

Depressed mood is the most common symptom, but it is not essential for diagnosis

VITAL FEELINGS:

Are somatic symptoms

Are automatic in origin

The head is the most common site of complaint

COENESTOPATHIC STATES:

Akin to vital feelings

Very common

Most frequent features of psychosis

Are distressing

Are localised

Are autonomous

Described by Dupre as associated with the affect of mood disturbance

Dupre, E. (1913). Les Cenestopathies, Mouvement Medical 3-22 (transl. Rohde, M. 1974). In Hirsch SR and Shepherd M (eds). Themes and Variations in European Psychiatry. Bristol: John Wright.

A RELIGIOUS FEELING IS NOT ASSOCIATED WITH MENTAL ILLNESS IF:

The patient is not too enthusiastic about discussing it with unbelievers

The feeling is authentic

The patient understands the incredulity of unbelievers

The patient considers the experience carries some demands on him

It conforms to peer group belief

RELIGIOUS FEELING IS ASSOCIATED WITH MENTAL ILLNESS IF:

The phenomenology conforms to mental illness

There are other symptoms of mental illness

The life course of the patient is consistent with the natural history of mental illness

There is disordered personality

REGARDING BIPOLAR DISORDER:

Depression occurs more frequently than mania

Usual course is depression, then mania, then depression, then normality (euthymia)

WITH DEPRESSION:

Anhedonia is a constant feature

Beck's triad includes a negative view of the self, a negative view of the world, and a negative view of the future

Beck, A., Rush, A., Shaw, B., Emery, G. (1987). Cognitive Therapy of Depression. Guildford Press

VULNERABILITY FACTORS FOR DEPRESSIVE ILLNESS INCLUDE:

Lack of close confidant

Loss of mother before age of 11

Three or more children younger than 15

Unemployment

Lack of support from partner

Low self-esteem

Brown, G. and Harris, T. (1978). Social Origins of Depression: A study of Psychiatric Disorder in Women. Tavistock: London.

SOME COGNITIVE DISTORTIONS OCCURRING IN DEPRESSION:

Arbitrary inference

Selective abstraction

Overgeneralisation

Minimisation and maximisation

THE FOLLOWING COULD OCCUR IN NORMAL GRIEF:

Depersonalisation

Denial

Anxious searching

Panic attacks

Depression

Pining for the lost object

Pseudohallucinations

THE FOLLOWING COULD OCCUR IN MORBID GRIEF:

Fearful avoidance

Extreme guilt and anger

A total lack of grief

Over-idealisation of the deceased

Physical illness

Recurrent nightmares of the deceased

ENGEL'S CHARACTERISTICS OF THE GIVING-UP—GIVEN-UP COMPLEX ARE:

Affect of hopelessness and helplessness

Loss of self-esteem

Loss of gratification in relationships and role in life

Disruption of the normal sense of continuity between the past, present, and future

Remembering prior occasions of lowered self-esteem

Engel, George L. (1968, August 1). A life setting conducive to illness. The giving-up—given-up complex. *Annals of Internal Medicine.* https://doi.org/10.7326/0003-4819-69-2-293

KRAEPELIN'S TRIAD OF MANIC-DEPRESSIVE PSYCHOSIS WILL OCCUR AT THREE LEVELS:

Mood: Too much or too little

Psychic activity: Presence of delusions and hallucinations that are congruent with the mood

Motor activity: Too little or too much

Kraepelin, E. (1921). Manic Depressive Insanity and Paranoia. Edinburgh: Livingstone.

SCHIZOAFFECTIVE PATIENTS:

Are young

Have acute onset of illness

Have good premorbid history

Have presence of external precipitants

Have presence of affective features

Have presence of Bleulerian criteria for schizophrenia (the four As)

DISORDERS OF CONSCIOUSNESS

THE THREE DIMENSIONS OF CONSCIOUSNESS:

Vigilance

Lucidity

Self-consciousness

UNCONSCIOUSNESS OCCURS IN:

Brain disease

Sleep

Healthy people who are unaware of some parts of their environment

ABOUT THE CONSCIOUS AND PRE-CONSCIOUS STATES:

The number of items available to the conscious state is 7 ± 2 items

Ambiguous information generates only one interpretation in consciousness

However, ambiguous information generates multiple interpretations in pre-consciousness

Pre-conscious processes are automatic

THE FOLLOWING ARE COMPONENTS OF CLOUDING OF CONSCIOUSNESS:

Deterioration of thinking

Deterioration of attention

Deterioration of perception

Deterioration of memory

All the above occur with reduced awareness of the environment

TWILIGHT STATES:

Occur in organic states

Are of abrupt onset and cessation

Can last from a few hours to several weeks

Violent behaviour may occur

Consciousness may or may not be impaired between episodes

Ganser state (syndrome of approximate answers, prison psychosis) is a sort of twilight state

AUTOMATISMS:

Acts performed in the absence of consciousness

There may be no memory or partial memory of acts

Occur in epilepsy

Violence is rare; when it occurs, it may be due to resistance to restraint

ONEIROID STATES:

Are dream-like states

Elaborate hallucinations occur, especially visual hallucinations

The hallucination may be enjoyable or may terrorise the patient

Occur in head injury, organic states, schizophrenia, and those in a dream world (occupational delirium)

STUPOR:

Akinesis (lack of movement)

Mutism (lack of speech)

No loss of consciousness, but impaired consciousness

Occurs in schizophrenia, affective psychosis, hysteria

Occurs in lesions of the diencephalon, brain stem, frontal lobe, and basal ganglia

THE FOUR COMPONENTS OF PATHOLOGICAL INTOXICATION (MANIA A POTU), ACCORDING TO COID, ARE:

Consumption of variable amount of alcohol

Violent behaviour

Prolonged sleep

Total or partial amnesia for the behaviour

Coid, J. (1979). Mania a potu: A critical review of pathological intoxication. Psychological Medicine, 9(4), 709-719.

PHOBIAS AND ANXIETIES

MARKS' FOUR CRITERIA FOR A PHOBIA ARE:

Fear out of proportion to demands of the situation

Cannot be explained or reasoned away

Not under voluntary control

Avoidance

Marks, I. (1987). *Fears, phobias, and rituals: Panic, anxiety, and their disorders*. New York: Oxford University Press.

THREE FEATURES FOR OBSESSIONS AND COMPULSIONS:

A feeling of subjective compulsion

A resistance to the feeling

The preservation of insight

OBSESSIONS TAKE THE FORM OF:

Thoughts

Images

Impulses

Ruminations

Fears

COMPULSIONS TAKE THE FORM OF:

Acts

Rituals

Behaviours

DE SILVA'S IMAGES OF OBSESSIONAL THINKING ARE:

The obsessional image

The compulsive image

The disaster image

The disruptive image

De Silva, P. (1986). Obsessional-compulsive imagery. *Behaviour Research and Therapy*, 24:3, pp 333–350.

OBSESSIONS AND COMPULSIONS:

When associated with schizophrenia, take bizarre character

There is no danger of homicide or suicide with ruminations

May be associated with depression if they disappear when the depression is treated

Are familial but there is no sharing of symptoms

EXPLANATIONS FOR OBSESSIONALITY INCLUDE:

Less tolerance or inability to tolerate ambiguity

Making of sweeping generalisations

Under-inclusive thinking

The sentiment of incompleteness

The patients are insecure, and sensitive and intolerant of uncertainty

THE THREE DISTINCT COMPONENTS OF THE ANANKASTIC PERSONALITY ARE:

Clean and tidy

Incompleteness

Checking

DEPERSONALISATION AND DEREALISATION

DEPERSONALISATION:

Is common

Is subjective

Is characterised by a feeling of strangeness

Is experienced as unpleasant in mentally ill people

Affect is always involved

Insight is preserved

DEPERSONALISATION:

Always occurs with derealisation

De-affectualisation may occur with it

May last from seconds to months

Is more often provoked

Distortion of time sense may occur

Is not pathognomonic of organic disease

DEPERSONALISATION DEREALISATION OCCUR IN:

Schizophrenia

Bipolar disorder, especially during the depressive phase

Anxiety

Organic mental states

Normal state

IN DEPERSONALISATION:

Anankastic personality disorder is a predisposing factor

The neuroticism score on the Eysenck Personality Inventory is raised

The four qualities of awareness are affected (activity, unity, identity, and boundary)

INTELLIGENCE

REGARDING INTELLIGENCE:

Thurstone considered primary abilities that are independent of each other

Spearman considered a general (g) factor in intelligence

Parents and biological children are 50% correlated in intelligence

Identical twins are 90% correlated in intelligence

Thurstone, L. L. (1938). Primary Mental Abilities. Psychometric monographs No. 1. Chicago: University of Chicago Press.

Spearman, C. E. (1927). The Abilities of Man: Their Nature and Measurement. London: Macmillan.

THE PRIMARY ABILITIES IN INTELLIGENCE ARE:

Verbal comprehension

Word fluency

Number

Space

Memory

Perceptual speed

Reasoning

THE g (GENERAL) FACTOR IN INTELLIGENCE IS A CONSTANT COMPRISING OF:

Fluid reasoning

Knowledge

Qualitative reasoning

Visual-spatial processing

Work memory

INTELLIGENCE CAN BE MEASURED BY:

Aptitude tests

Achievement tests

Wechsler Adult Intelligence Scale (WAIS)

Wechsler Intelligence Scale for Children (WISC)

Mental age scale by Binet

IQ tests

WAIS AND WISC:

Measure verbal IQ and performance IQ between the ages of 5–15 years

Total test item is 11

Performance has five items

Verbal has six items

CONTENTS OF PERFORMANCE TEST:

Picture completion

Block design

Picture arrangement

Object assembly

Digit symbol

CONTENTS OF THE VERBAL TEST ARE:

Information

Comprehension

Arithmetic

Similarities

Digital span

Vocabulary

DISORDERS OF THE SELF

THE CHARACTERISTICS OF SELF-AWARENESS ACCORDING TO JASPERS ARE:

The feeling of awareness of activity

An awareness of unity

An awareness of identity

An awareness of boundary of self

Jaspers, K. (1963). General Psychopathology 7th. Edition. Hoenig. J. and Hamilton, M. W. Manchester: Manchester University Press. (Original work published 1959)

THE DISORDERS OF AWARENESS OF UNITY ARE:

Autoscopy

The double phenomenon

Multiple personality

MULTIPLE PERSONALITY:

Could be conscious and deliberate in children

It is rare in adults

One-way amnesia is usual

The forms commonly seen are simultaneous partial personalities, successive well-defined personalities, and clustered multiple partial personalities

DISORDERED IDENTITY COULD OCCUR IN:

Schizophrenia

Organic states

Neurotic states

Affective states

Healthy people during possession states

THE FOLLOWING COULD OCCUR IN NEAR-DEATH EXPERIENCES:

Depersonalisation

Hyper alertness

Autoscopy

Transcendental experience

DISTURBANCE OF AWARENESS OF BOUNDARY OF SELF IN SCHIZOPHRENIA MANIFESTS AS:

Passivity phenomena

Third-person auditory hallucinations

Thought echo

Delusional percept

THE FOLLOWING PHENOMENA OCCUR IN NEUROSIS:

Total absorption with self

All-pervading fear of loss of self

Anxiety in relationships

Withdrawal from close personal contact

"Black and white" view of the world

Lack of competence and self-doubting

THE EGO:

Has three masters: the external world, the superego, and the id

According to Freud, the ego is firstly the body ego

Enhancement, distortion and ablation can alter the body image

Stands for reason and good sense according to Freud

DISORDERS OF MEMORY

REGARDING MEMORY:

Duration of sensory memory is less than 1 second (0.5 s)

There is a separate iconic and echoic storage for sensory memory

Duration of short-term memory is 15–30 seconds (30 s)

The capacity of short-term memory is 7 ± 2 items

Memories of words are retained as sounds in short-term memory

Verbal memory is in located the left hemisphere of the brain

LONG-TERM MEMORY:

Lasts a few minutes to many decades

The capacity is large

Storage is semantic

Forgetting may occur by loss of information or failure of retrieval

Types include semantic and episodic memory

MEMORY MECHANISMS ARE:

Registration

Retention

Retrieval

Recall

Recognition

COMPONENTS OF APPERCEPTION INCLUDE THE ABILITY TO:

Understand what is perceived

Interpret what is perceived

Form associations between perceptions

Incorporate perceptions into total experience

FAILURE OF REGISTRATION:

Is a symptom par excellence of delirium tremens

Occurs in anterograde amnesia following head injury

Occurs in alcoholic palimpsest

Occurs in the absence of apperception

FAILURE OF RETENTION:

May occur in immediate, recent, and remote memory

Unilateral lobectomy leads to no impairment in retention

Temporal lobectomy leads to impairment of recent memory

Failure of recent memory occurs early in dementia

Failure of recent memory occurs in retrograde amnesia of head injury

Hypnosis and intravenous barbiturates can improve memory for events before the head injury

CONCERNING RETRIEVAL DEFICITS:

Diencephalic and hippocampal amnesia are pure forms of retrieval deficits

In diencephalic amnesia (Korsakov's), there is lack of insight, denial of disability, and confabulation

In hippocampal amnesia, insight and judgment are unaffected, and there is no confabulation because there is impairment of relational memory, which consists of spatial, associative and sequential aspects

CONFABULATIONS:

Falsification of memory in clear consciousness

Suggestibility is a prominent feature

There is no confabulation in severe Korsakov syndrome

Are actual experiences taken out of their chronological order; it is not lying

REGARDING MEMORY DEFICITS:

Memory deficit that is associated with perseveration is pathognomonic of brain disease

Anterograde and retrograde amnesia occur as a side effect of electroconvulsive therapy (ECT)

Unilateral, non-dominant ECT gives rise to fewer memory deficits

TEMPORAL LOBE MEMORY DISTURBANCE:

Reduced storage

Increased forgetting

Déjà-vu and jamais-vu

Fugue states occur

Panoramic recall of information can occur

BIBLIOGRAPHY

1. Jaspers, K. (1963). *General Psychopathology*, 7th edition (J. Hoenig and M. W. Hamilton, Trans.). Manchester: Manchester University Press. (Original work published 1959)
2. Sims, A. (1995). *Symptoms in the Mind*, 2nd edition. London: WB Saunders Company Ltd.

ABOUT THE AUTHOR

Dr Daniel Chinedu Okoro graduated with a Bachelor of Medicine, Bachelor of Surgery (MB. BS) degree from the University of Lagos, Lagos, Nigeria. After completing his psychiatric rotational training posts in the United Kingdom, he immigrated to Canada in 2000. He successfully passed both the Licentiate of the Medical Council of Canada (LMCC) and Fellowship of the Royal College of Physicians of Canada (FRCPC) examinations, both required for foreign-trained doctors to practise in Canada at the time. In 2006, he passed the American Board of Psychiatry and Neurology examination, becoming American Board Certified.

Dr Okoro has an abiding interest in the practice of psychiatry in rural settings, delivering psychiatric services to disadvantaged populations, such as Black people, Indigenous people, other people of colour, LGBTQ people, and homeless urban people. In the heat of the Afghan war, with the consequent epidemic in military suicides, Dr Okoro volunteered to be contracted as a civilian psychiatrist to the Canadian Forces. He served in a remote military base for three years, and during this period his unique approach to treating suicidal patients reduced the suicide occurrence to zero in this base.

Dr Okoro firmly believes that psychiatric training today must chart a different trajectory with the inculcation of cultural psychiatry in the curriculum. He is enthusiastic in welcoming medical students, psychiatric residents, and other trainees into his rural and Indigenous mental health clinics. He emphasises the interface of psychiatric phenomenology and culture. Dr. Okoro is a clinical assistant professor in the department of Psychiatry, University of Calgary.

For relaxation, Dr Okoro plays golf, plays the conga drums very well, and is a jazz buff.

Dr Okoro has been elected a Fellow of the American Psychiatric Association (FAPA).

www.ingramcontent.com/pod-product-compliance
Lightning Source LLC
LaVergne TN
LVHW042000060526
838200LV00041B/1810